Happy Eating!
Madeline Wellereune

Enjoy
Alexa Rom

Happy Entertaining!
♡ Tania Ferran

have fun!
Annika Jamm

THE EYES EAT FIRST!
Kit

Easy Entertaining: Hosting Made Easy

Copyright © 2020 by Tania M. Farran

All rights reserved. No part of this book may be reproduced or used in any manner without written permission of the copyright owner.
For more information, address: taniafarran@creativelivingideas.com

Written by Tania Farran
Book design by Kristen Landon, Maddie Villeneuve, Alexis Romeril
Contributions by Annika Farran
Edited by Maddie Villeneuve and Michele Dunaway

Published by Creative Living Ideas
ISBN: 978-1-7363567-0-8

www.creativelivingideas.com

Dedication

Thank you to my family for working hard during this difficult time. Thank you for making such wonderful memories. Contributors for this edition were:

    Ron Farran

    Annika Farran

    Alexis Romeril

    Arren Romeril

    Kristen Landon

    Maddie Villeneuve

I dedicate this book to my family. They are such an important part of my life. Without their enthusiasm and support, this book would not have been possible. My family embraced every game night that you will read about in this book. The nights we spent together brought us all closer together and helped to lighten our hearts during a trying time. Thank you to my beautiful family for making this pandemic bearable. It was your love and support that made this book possible.

I also dedicate this book to our essential workers, especially our healthcare workers who are taking care of others. Please know that I do not take this pandemic lightly by playing games and having dinner parties. It is merely how I am coping with this situation. I know that those of you on the frontline are working tirelessly to save lives and come up with treatments. As a result, you are sacrificing time with your family. I pray daily for your safety and for the safety of our world. Thank you.

Finally, thank you to my Creative Living Ideas Team for working diligently to get *Easy Entertaining* completed. I truly appreciate your gifts and talent. You have been amazing to work with on this project. I am looking forward to completing future projects together.

Table of Contents

Before Your Guests Arrive – 06

The Beginning – 08

Easy Italian Feast – 11

Hometown Hoagie – 14

Everyday Thanksgiving – 19

Couch Potato Cuisine – 23

American Made – 27

The Middle – 30

A Trip East – 33

A Taste of Ireland – 37

Backyard BBQ – 41

Breakfast for Dinner – 45

Southwestern Staycation – 49

The End – 52

Alternate Recipes – 54

Before Your Arrive Guests

Two Weeks

At least two weeks prior to the party, assemble your guest list and send out the invitations. These can be sent out in the mail or as a simple text message. Once that's complete, choose the theme for the party. This is my favorite part; don't be afraid to get creative! The theme is important because it will help guide your menu, decor, and entertainment for the evening.

Two Days

Create a grocery list and stick to it. Make sure to grab a few extra snack items to put out if you run low on food. Plan and gather decorations that match the theme. Make sure to clue your guests in on the theme so they are prepared to come in costume if desired. Double check that you have all of the necessary materials for any game you plan on playing.

One Day

Prepare your home for guests. Choose a space to play the game. I like to choose a different area than where we are eating dinner so that I don't have to flip an entire room. Don't stress about cleaning uneccessary areas. Clean the spaces you are using and the nearest bathroom. I promise your guests will not run to see if your closets are cleaned out.

Three Hours

Begin decorating the house to match the theme. The atmosphere is what keeps guests coming back. If you're having a dinner party, light some candles and dim the lights. Select quiet music to play in the background. Music will set the tone, and it's usually the first thing guests will notice when they walk in. The music can correspond to the theme as well.

Two Hours

Start preparing the food! Try to complete all of your prep work, such as cleaning and chopping vegetables, beforehand. Prepare appetizers first so that you can clean that up while the main course is cooking. If this is a potluck, make sure to have space in the kitchen for each guest's dish. Decide if you want to use paper products or real dishes and have those set out.

Party Time!

Enjoy the evening with your guests! Once the party starts, do not spend time stressing out about dirty dishes or dust on the mantel. Spend time with your guests, laugh, and make notes of what you want to change for the next party. To eliminate stress, make sure to have a stock of ice, cups, and drinks. They are easy to store and will eliminate emergency drink runs.

The Beginning

For me, entertaining comes easy. My home has always been the center of every celebration, birthday, holiday, and event for our family. Whether it was a princess-themed birthday party, or a family Christmas gathering, I was always the hostess. My love for entertaining is the inspiration behind this book.

However, entertaining would be much less meaningful without my family. I have been married to my husband, Ron, for 30 years. We grew up in the Midwest, and we became high school sweethearts when we first met. We live in the same house Ron grew up in as a child. We have two daughters, Lexi and Anni. Both of my children inherited my love of entertaining. Lexi is married to Arren, who has quickly become part of the family.

During the pandemic of 2020, I spent a lot of time cooking to keep my mind busy. I have always loved to cook, so I decided to go through some of my old cookbooks while I had the time. This book evolved out of the meals I cooked each night. After dinner, we would play a game and spend quality time together. It was the perfect way to keep our minds off what was happening in the world. Eventually, the evenings turned into themed dinners and entertainment challenges.

My hope is for you to get creative with your cooking and to improve the quality of your family time. Life is precious, so make the most of it when you have the opportunity. When I created this book, I did it with the belief that entertaining can be simple and stress free. This book will share ideas for an evening's dinner and entertainment. The ideas are perfect for a weekday family night or an intimate dinner party. I hope that you are inspired to focus on family, food, and fun.

Italian Martini

2 ounces vodka
1/2 ounce dry vermouth
Olive juice
Olives

Add two scoops of ice to a cocktail shaker. Pour in vodka and vermouth. Add olive juice to taste. Shake, then strain into a martini glass. Garnish with olives. Makes one serving.

Night One: Easy Italian Feast

Baked Spaghetti

1 box (16 ounces) dry spaghetti
1 pound bulk Italian sausage
1½ - 2 jars spaghetti sauce
1 teaspoon Italian seasoning
1 teaspoon garlic powder
⅓ cup heavy cream
6 slices provolone cheese
½ cup parmesan cheese

Brown the Italian sausage in a large skillet. Drain the grease. Add the spaghetti sauce and seasonings to the browned sausage. Bring to a boil and then simmer on low for 20 minutes. While this is simmering, boil the dry spaghetti in a four-quart pot of salted water. Add the heavy cream to the sauce. Drain the spaghetti and add to the meat sauce. Stir the spaghetti and sauce together.

Add ½ of the spaghetti mixture to the 9 x 13 pan and sprinkle with parmesan cheese. Add the rest of the spaghetti and sprinkle with parmesan cheese. Cover and bake at 350 degrees for 15 minutes. Uncover and add provolone slices. Bake until the cheese melts, about 5 minutes. Do not overbrown. Remove, let stand 5 minutes and serve.

Planning Ahead

Baked Spaghetti
Prep Time: 30 minutes
Cook Time: 25 minutes
Servings: 5-6

Tiramisu
Prep Time: 4-6 hours
Servings: 8-10

Tiramisu, inspired by *Rosalie Serving Best Loved Italian* by Rosalie Fiorino Harpole

1½ cup coffee, cooled
¼ cup sugar

8 egg yolks
¾ cup sugar

1 cup heavy whipping cream
¼ cup sugar

40 Italian ladyfinger cookies
2 teaspoons brandy
2 packages (8 ounces) Mascarpone cheese, softened
1 chocolate candy bar, grated
Cocoa powder

Combine the coffee and sugar. Stir until sugar is dissolved. Set aside.

To make the custard, mix egg yolks with an electric mixer adding the sugar a little at a time. Mix on low for 8-10 minutes or until it forms a custard. Set aside.

For the whipped topping, mix heavy whipping cream and sugar with an electric mixer on low until it forms stiff peaks. Add the brandy and two packages of Mascarpone cheese. Mix until thick. Fold the custard into the whipped topping.

Layer a 9 x 13 pan with ladyfinger cookies (about 15). Spoon ½ of the coffee mixture onto and over the ladyfingers. Spoon and spread the custard/whipped topping over the top of the ladyfingers. Sprinkle with the candy bar shavings and cocoa powder. Create the second layer by dipping ladyfingers into the coffee. Put dipped ladyfingers on top of the custard/whipped topping. Spoon and spread the remaining custard/whipped topping over the second layer of ladyfingers. Sprinkle with candy bar shavings and cocoa.

Top with store bought whipped topping if you choose. Garnish with chocolate and cocoa powder. Refrigerate 4-6 hours or overnight.

Chicken Foot

Chicken Foot (dominoes)
Pad of paper and pen for scoring

Play begins with 7 dominoes. Players continue to draw until someone has a double 0. Each player plays on their own domino line, beginning with a 0. Playing a double domino is called chicken foot. If you do not have a domino to play on your own line, you must draw or put up your chicken. By putting up your chicken, your turn is skipped and other players can place their dominoes in your line. Once a player has placed all the domines, that round is over. The goal is to have the least amount of points.

Tania Tip

Before play gets started, arrange your dominoes numerically to stay organized.

15 minutes **4-6** players

Night Two: Hometown Hoagie

Italian Beef

4-5 pounds chuck roast
½ - 1 cup water
2 beef bouillon cubes
2 tablespoons Italian seasoning
1 teaspoon garlic powder
1 teaspoon onion powder
Salt and pepper
1 jar (12 ounces) banana pepper rings

In a slow cooker, add water, bouillon cubes, and chuck roast. Sprinkle the seasonings and banana pepper rings over top. Cover and cook 5-6 hours on low (if frozen, cook 7-8 hours on low). Remove the beef from the slow cooker. On a cutting board, shred the beef and place back into the juice.

Serve on a hoagie or pretzel bun. Add your favorite condiments. Use the juice like an Au Jus for dipping if desired.

Gooey Butter Cake, inspired by *Rosalie Serving Best Loved Italian* by Rosalie Fiorino Harpole

1 box yellow cake mix
4 large eggs
1 stick butter or margarine, softened
2 teaspoons vanilla extract
1 package (8 ounces) cream cheese, softened
4 cups powdered sugar

Preheat the oven to 350 degrees. Grease a 9 x 13 baking dish. Mix together the cake mix, 2 eggs, butter, and 1 teaspoon vanilla extract. Spread mixture into the baking dish-it will be thick. Make sure that it reaches the edges of the dish.

In a clean bowl, mix together the cream cheese, remaining 2 eggs, and remaining vanilla extract. Then, add the powdered sugar 1 cup at a time. Mix until smooth. Pour on top of the cake batter. Bake for 35 minutes or until the top is lightly browned. Cool and sprinkle with powdered sugar.

Planning Ahead

Italian Beef
- Prep Time: 5 minutes
- Cook Time: 6-7 hours
- Servings: 5-6

Gooey Butter Cake
- Prep Time: 15-20 minutes
- Cook Time: 35 minutes
- Servings: 12-16

Midwestern Mule

2 ounces vodka or gin
1 ounce lime juice
5 ounces ginger beer
Fresh berries
Fresh mint

Combine vodka or gin with lime juice and ginger beer. Garnish with fresh berries and a sprig of mint. Makes one serving.

Blackjack

Deck of playing cards
Poker chips or coins

You want to either get Blackjack (21) or at least get closer to 21 than the dealer does, without going over. An ace can be used as 1 or 11, face cards are 10, and any other card is used as its numbered value. We used chips, created our own point values, and set our minimum bet at $5. When all the players have placed their bets, the dealer gives one card face up to everyone, including themselves. Another round of cards is then dealt face up to each player, but the dealer takes their second card face down.

If a player is dealt an ace and a face card or 10, making 21, they hit Blackjack and win their own hand. If the dealer has Blackjack, they immediately collect the players' bets who do not have it. If the dealer and another player both have 21, it's a tie and the player may take back their chips. One by one, the players decide whether to "stay" (not ask for another card) or "hit" (ask for another card in an attempt to get closer to a count of 21). The player may also "bust" (if they go over 21). In that case, the player loses, and the dealer collects the bet. This continues for each player.

TaniaTip

You don't have to have a poker set to play this game. You can use anything as chips (pennies, pretzels, etc.).

30+ minutes **2+ players**

Fiery Hot Toddy

2 ounces cinnamon whiskey
4 ounces hot apple cider
1 cinnamon stick

Warm the apple cider, whiskey, and cinnamon stick in a saucepan. Pour the hot toddy in a mug. Makes one serving.

Night Three: Everyday Thanksgiving

Roasted Turkey

12-15 pound turkey
Salt and pepper
Vegetable oil
2 teaspoons garlic powder
2 teaspoons dried parsley
4 celery stalks, diced
1 white onion, diced
2 carrots, diced

If frozen, thaw turkey according to the instructions on the package (can take up to a week in the refrigerator). Once thawed, clean and rinse the turkey. Remove the neck and bagged items from inside the turkey. Put the turkey in a roasting pan. Rub vegetable oil on the outside of the turkey. Sprinkle with salt, pepper, garlic powder, and parsley and rub all over the outside of the skin and inside the cavity.

Dice the celery, onion, and carrots. Place inside the cavity of the turkey. Once prepared, cook in the oven according to the weight of the turkey. A good rule of thumb is to cook 20 minutes per pound at 325 degrees or until the internal temperature of the turkey is 165 degrees.

Planning Ahead

Roasted Turkey
  Prep Time: 15-20 minutes
  Cook Time: 5-6 hours
  Servings: 8-10

Arren's Cheesy Potatoes
  Prep Time: 10 minutes
  Cook Time: 10-15 minutes
  Servings: 4-5

Pumpkin Dump Cake
  Prep Time: 10-15 minutes
  Cook Time: 1 hour
  Servings: 5-6

Arren's Cheesy Potatoes

4-5 Yukon gold potatoes
2-3 tablespoons butter
2-3 tablespoons olive oil
2 teaspoons Montreal steak seasoning
½ cup colby-jack cheese, shredded

Leaving the peel on, dice the potatoes into ½ inch cubes. Heat olive oil in a skillet, add the butter, and add the potatoes once the butter has melted. Cook over medium heat until potatoes are soft.

Sprinkle the Montreal steak seasoning over the potatoes. Add the cheese. Stir and heat until cheese is melted.

Pumpkin Dump Cake

1 can (30 ounces) pumpkin
1 can (16 ounces) evaporated milk
2 teaspoons pumpkin pie spice
1 cup sugar
4 eggs
1 box yellow cake mix
1 cup pecans, chopped
1 stick butter
1 carton whipped topping

Mix together the pumpkin, evaporated milk, pumpkin pie spice, sugar, and eggs. Pour into a greased 9 x 13 pan. Sprinkle cake mix over the top. Then, sprinkle on chopped pecans over the cake mix. Melt a stick of butter and drizzle over the top.

Bake at 350 degrees for 50-60 minutes or until a toothpick comes out clean when stuck in the middle of the cake. Let cool and slice. Top with whipped topping.

Garbage

Decks of playing cards

This game for two to three players uses a 52-card deck (additional decks are needed for four or more players). The object of the game is to be the first player to line up your cards in a sequence starting with the ace. To start, deal 10 cards to each player. The remaining deck is placed in the middle. As each player draws a card, they can place it in the correct order from ace to 10, replacing cards until they cannot place a card in sequence. That card then goes in the discard pile.

Kings are wild cards and can be used as any number. If another player has a discard that you can use, it can be played for your turn. The goal is to have all 10 of the cards face up in the correct order. Play continues this way, with winning players going down one card, and losing players replaying with the same number of cards as the previous round. The first player to flip an ace in their last round wins the game.

Wine Spritzer

5 ounces red wine
3 ounces Sprite™
Fresh berries

Mix the wine and Sprite™ in a glass with ice. Add berries for a colorful, delicious garnish. Makes one serving.

Night Four: Couch Potato Cuisine

Chicken Gnocchi with Butternut Squash and Kale

4-5 chicken breasts, thawed and cubed
Salt and pepper
1 teaspoon garlic, minced
1 butternut squash, peeled and cubed
1½ cups kale, loosely packed
12 ounces potato gnocchi
1 tablespoon olive oil
2 tablespoons unsalted butter
1 cup heavy whipping cream
½ cup parmesan cheese

Heat the olive oil and 1 tablespoon butter in a large, nonstick pan. Add the chicken and sprinkle with salt and pepper. Sauté until the chicken is lightly browned and cooked through. Remove chicken from the pan and set aside.

Bring a four-quart pot of water to a boil. Add the gnocchi and cook until they float to the top. Drain and set aside.

While the gnocchi cooks, add the squash, remaining butter, and garlic to the same pan you used for the chicken. Sauté on medium heat for about 8 minutes. Add the kale and sauté for 2 minutes. Turn the heat down to low and add the cream and parmesan cheese to the pan and stir until the sauce thickens. In a serving bowl, gently mix the gnocchi, chicken, and vegetable mixture. Serve.

Planning Ahead

Chicken Gnocchi with Butternut Squash and Kale
Prep Time: 5-10 minutes
Cook Time: 30-45 minutes
Servings: 4-5

Arren's Trifle Cups
Prep Time: 8-10 hours
Servings: 5-6

Arren's Trifle Cups

1 package strawberry Jell-O™
1 package orange Jell-O™
2 cups Bird's Custard™
6 angel food cake rounds
Strawberries, sliced
Oranges, peeled and sliced
Kiwi, peeled and sliced
6 tablespoons brandy
1 carton whipped topping

Place 1 angel food cake round in the bottom of 6 ramekins. Add 1 tablespoon of flavored brandy to each cake and let it soak into the cakes.

In a separate bowl, mix the strawberry Jell-O™ according to package instructions. Let the Jell-O™ set for an hour, but make sure that the Jell-O™ has not fully set. Scoop the strawberry Jell-O™ into the ramekins. Top with strawberries and oranges or whatever fresh fruit you have on hand. Put in the fridge for 4-6 hours until the Jell-O™ is fully set.

Following the directions on the box, mix together the custard and let it cool for 30 minutes. Add the custard to the ramekins. Put in the fridge for 1-2 hours. Mix the orange Jell-O™ according to package instructions. Let set for 1 hour. Add the orange Jell-O™ to the ramekins. Top with kiwi. Put in the fridge for another 4-6 hours. Just before serving, add the whipped topping and garnish with fruit.

Fibbage

Smart TV or a device to plug into the TV, such as a Firestick
Personal phone devices
Wi-Fi

We gathered in the living area of the cottage and played Fibbage. It is a game of tricking and bluffing one another. You play from a Web browser. You can go to fibbage.com to get directions to the game. Be prepared to pay a small fee for game access.

TaniaTip

Make sure that everyone has a fully charged phone and a comfy place to sit before beginning play.

15+ minutes 2+ players

Gin and Tonic

2 ounces gin
3 ounces tonic water
Fresh mint

Pour the gin and tonic water into a glass filled with ice. Add a sprig of fresh mint as a garnish. Makes one serving.

Night Five: American Made

Sirloin Steaks

5-6 Sirloin steaks
2 tablespoons Montreal steak seasoning

Set steaks out until they get to room temperature. Poke 5-6 holes in each steak with a knife. Rub the Montreal steak seasoning into the meat.

Heat the grill to 350 degrees. Put the steaks on the grill and cook for 7 minutes. Flip the steaks and cook on the other side for 7 minutes. Cooking times may vary depending on the desired temperature. Remove the meat from the grill, and let it rest for a few minutes before serving. Serve with your favorite sides.

Anni's Pudding Cake

1 store-bought chocolate Bundt cake
8 chocolate pudding cups
Sprinkles

Cut the Bundt cake in half lengthwise (like a top and bottom). Carve a trough out of the bottom of the cake to make a spot for the pudding. Scoop the pudding from 8 pudding cups into the bottom of the cake until it is oozing out of the cake. Gently put the top of the cake back on top of the pudding. Sprinkle red, white, and blue sprinkles on the top. Chill for 1-2 hours. Slice and serve!

Planning Ahead

Sirloin Steaks
Prep Time: 25 minutes
Cook Time: 15 minutes
Servings: 5-6

Anni's Pudding Cake
Prep Time: 1-2 hours
Servings: 6-8

Family Feud™

Buzzer
Name tags
Question cards

Anni broke out her game of Family Feud™ cards and served as the host. You can purchase this game or find trivia questions online. Anni also created name tags similar to those on a game show. The name tags served as our seat place cards for dinner. It was The Farrans versus The Romerils. Anni read the questions from the cards and tallied the answers. She dug out her old iCarly™ recorded sound box, which has the sound effects of booing and cheering. This addition led to lots of laughs during the game. We also played bonus rounds, which we improvised by selecting specific questions and increasing the point total from 200 to 300 per game. We played a few rounds and had a blast.

TaniaTip

Make your place setting unique by using the contestant name tags as place cards at the dinner table.

30+ minutes **2+ players**

- RON
- TANIA
- ARREN
- EXI
- ANNI

The Middle

If your family is like mine, you may often hear an enthusiastic (and nightly), "What's for dinner tonight?" In my house, that question was usually followed by another, "What should we do this evening?" During the COVID-19 pandemic especially, we all needed laughter, light-heartedness, and a bit of competition. So, here is where our evenings began to evolve.

I suggested that we create teams to plan the dinner and entertainment for certain nights of the week. The rules were that teams could use any of the food, dishes, and props that were in our house. Teams had three days to plan and complete the challenge.

As the days progressed, teams became increasingly excited about their upcoming challenge. Everyone was looking up recipes for inspiration and being secretive about their plans. This secrecy piqued the family's curiosity. On my end, I was thrilled that I didn't have to think about dinner for that night. I was excited to see what was being planned by each team. It turned out to be an amazing time for all of us.

Planning Ahead

Lettuce Wraps
Prep Time: 20 minutes
Cook Time: 15 minutes
Servings: 5-6

Anni's Turkey Sliders
Prep Time: 10 minutes
Cook Time: 15 minutes
Servings: 5-6

Night Six: A Trip East

Lettuce Wraps

1 pound ground turkey
English cucumber, sliced
Carrots, julienned
Bell peppers, julienned
Romaine lettuce

Teriyaki Sauce
½ cup soy sauce
½ cup brown sugar, packed

Lettuce Wraps
Brown the ground turkey in a skillet until fully cooked. Add the teriyaki sauce. Clean each leaf of lettuce and top with the prepared ground turkey. Serve with peppers, carrots, and cucumbers for guests to add to their own portion.

Teriyaki Sauce
Mix the soy sauce and brown sugar in a saucepan. Cook over medium heat until the sugar has dissolved and the sauce has thickened. Add to the ground turkey. Serve with the lettuce wraps as a glaze or dipping sauce.

Cucumber Vodka Water

2 ounces vodka
4 ounces water
4 cucumber slices

Pour the vodka and water into a glass filled with ice. Put 3 slices of cucumber in the glass and use the remaining slice for garnish on the rim. Makes one serving.

Anni's Turkey Sliders

1 pound ground turkey
Salt and pepper
1 teaspoon garlic powder
Olive oil (if needed)
American cheese
Hawaiian rolls

Mix the ground turkey with the salt, pepper, and garlic powder. Shape into 10-12 small, slider-size burgers. Fry in a skillet until the burgers are fully cooked. You may need to add a bit of olive oil to the pan if the ground turkey is really lean. Melt slices of American cheese on top of the burgers and place each slider on a Hawaiian roll.

🔍 Dr. Farran

🔍 Mr. Maple Licker

Rules

1. Roll a "6" or a "3"
2. Each player proceeds one at a time
3. Go to a room in the house to look for a clue envelope and mark the clue on your sheet
4. If you find a pink "Sneak a Peek" card, keep it, you may use it at any turn in the game. The Sneak takes one whole turn.
5. When you have an assumption, call it out. Check the Top Secret folder. If you're right, YOU WIN! If you're wrong, you're disqualified.

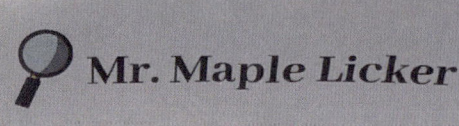
TOP SECRET

🔍 Professor Podcast

Sneak a Peek
You have found a sneak a peek card!
You may use this to ask
ONE PLAYER FOR ONE CLUE.
Ex. Ask a player about one thing in secret,
Like, "Have you found the candlestick?"

🔍 The Bank Teller

🔍 Colonel Mustard Stain

Clue™ (Dinner Party version)

Dice
Images of weapons printed
Names of characters and rooms printed

Envelopes
Sheet with the character names, weapons, and rooms (for participants to fill in)

We came up with silly names for our family members' game characters. Below are the names that we used:
- Lexi: Professor Podcast
- Arren: Mr. Maple Licker
- Ron: Colonel Mustard Stain
- Tania: Dr. Farran
- Anni: Bank Teller
- Rocko, our dog: Rocko Bing Bong
- Nelly, Lexi's dog: Smelly Nelly
- Luci, Anni's dog: Scaredy Luci

Lexi created various symbols for eight weapons, eight rooms, and eight people. One person, one room, and one weapon were placed in the "TOP SECRET" envelope. Then, the envelope was sealed shut. Lexi put all of the clues separately in envelopes and hid them in different rooms of the house. If you rolled a 3 or 6, you were able to go find a clue in a room. If you did not roll a 3 or 6, you had to sit and wait for your turn to come around again. Once you found a clue, you checked it off your list. Using the process of elimination, you could make an educated guess about the contents of the "TOP SECRET" envelope. This continued until someone thought they could solve the murder mystery. Can you believe that Rocko Bing Bong used the rope in the bathroom?

Tania Tip

You can't overdo this game-- Make sure you are dressing and acting to match your player's name.

30+ minutes   2+ players

Planning Ahead

Tater Tot Shepherd's Pie
  Prep Time: 30-45 minutes
  Cook Time: 40-45 minutes
  Servings: 6-8

Garden Salad
  Prep Time: 5-10 minutes
  Servings: 1

Night Seven: Taste of Ireland

Tater Tot Shepherd's Pie

2 pounds ground beef
1 bag (32 ounces) frozen tater tots
1 bag (16 ounces) frozen green beans
4-5 Yukon gold potatoes
½ stick butter
½ cup milk
1 can cream of mushroom soup
1 teaspoon garlic powder
1 cup colby-jack cheese, shredded
Salt and pepper

Brown beef in a skillet and drain the grease. Add soup, garlic, salt, and pepper to the beef. Then, in a greased 9 x 13 baking dish, place frozen tater tots on the bottom. Add the beef and frozen green beans. Peel the potatoes and boil them until tender. Drain, then add butter and milk. Salt and pepper to taste. Mash the potatoes to the consistency that you like. Spread mashed potatoes on top of the green beans and sprinkle with cheese. Bake at 350 degrees for 40-45 minutes.

Garden Salad

4 leaves Romaine lettuce
¼ cucumber, diced
¼ bell pepper, diced
¼ carrot, diced
⅛ cup colby-jack cheese, shredded
2 tablespoons Italian dressing

Wash and chop lettuce, peppers, cucumber, and carrots. Lay the lettuce on the bottom and top with peppers, cucumbers, and carrots. Sprinkle with shredded cheese. This recipe is great to make ahead for lunches. Without the cheese, it stays fresh for about 4-5 days. Add grilled chicken for added protein.

Jameson and Ginger Ale

1 ounce Jameson Irish Whiskey™
4-6 ounces ginger ale
Two lime wedges

Fill half of the glass with ice. Add the shot of Jameson™. Add the ginger ale, leaving some room at the top of the glass. Stir the drink, then squeeze in the juice of the lime wedges. Makes one serving.

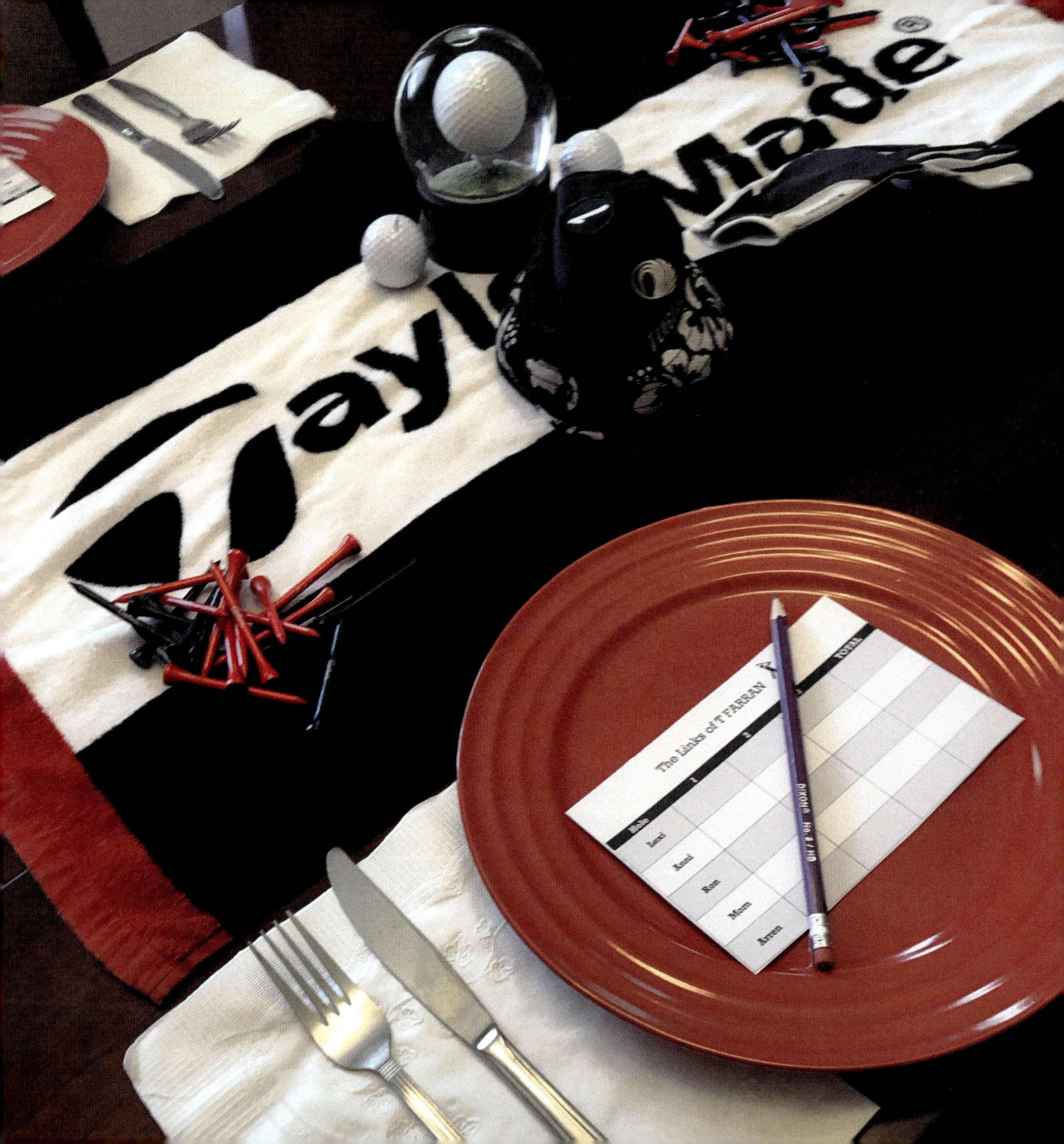

Golf-A-Round

Score cards
Golf clubs, including irons, wedges, and putters
Whiffle balls
Golf balls
Paper plates
Markers
Pencils
Sticks or wooden skewers
Construction paper
PVC pipe/old gutter
Wooden boards

Arren and I were partners for this challenge, so we decided to create a backyard golf course. We divided the backyard up into three sections: chipping, driving, and putting.

Chipping

We created four chipping sections in the yard, each with a point value. By making a small flag out of a stick, a piece of paper, and a paper plate, we were able to create a target to chip the ball onto.

Longest Drive

Arren and I marked off a tee box with whiffle ball bats. Then, we hit large whiffle balls with either a driver or a wedge. Once each person hit the ball, they went out and marked their ball with their assigned marker. Point values were given to each person. The value decreased from the longest drive to the shortest (i.e., 20, 15, 10, 5, 0).

Putt-Putt

We found a downhill section of our yard and different objects around the house to create a putt-putt challenge. We outlined this portion of the course with wood 2 x 4's. We added obstacles in the middle of the course, including a large rock, an old tire swing, and a broken gutter. A putt-putt stroke of 10+ scored 0 points, 9 scored 3 points, and so on.

TaniaTip

Adjust the level of difficulty based on the experience of the players.

30+ minutes   2+ players

Summertime Blues

1 ounce Whipped Vodka™
6 ounces water
4 squirts blue raspberry Mio™
1 orange, sliced

Add vodka, water, and Mio™ to a mason jar. Stir to combine. Garnish with a slice of orange. Makes one serving.

Night Eight: Backyard BBQ

St. Louis-Style Pork Steaks

5-6 pork steaks
BBQ sauce (Use your family's favorite)
2 tablespoons Montreal steak seasoning

Remove the pork steaks from the packaging. Prepare them in a 9 x 13 baking dish by sprinkling a generous amount of Montreal steak seasoning on the meat. Rub into the pork steaks. Let them sit while you start the grill.

Cook the pork until the outside is done and the meat is firm. Brush with BBQ sauce while on the grill. Put pork steaks in a prepared pan, pour more BBQ sauce over the top, and cover with foil. Put it in the oven at 200 degrees for a few hours. The pork steaks need to simmer in the sauce to become tender.

Planning Ahead

St. Louis-Style Pork Steaks
    Prep Time: 10-15 minutes
    Cook Time: 2-3 hours
    Servings: 5-6

Lexi's Baked Mac and Cheese
    Prep Time: 20 minutes
    Cook Time: 25-30 minutes
    Servings: 6-8

Lexi's Baked Mac and Cheese

1 box (16 ounces) dry macaroni
½ cup milk
2 ⅓ cups colby-jack cheese, shredded
½ stick butter or margarine
⅓ cup flour
⅓ cup breadcrumbs

Boil water and cook macaroni noodles according to the directions on the box.

In a separate saucepan, melt the butter and add the flour, stirring constantly. Add the milk and continue to stir until heated. Add 2 cups of shredded cheese, continuing to stir. Once the cheese is melted, add the cooked macaroni noodles to the pan.

Pour into a greased 9 x 13 pan. Sprinkle the breadcrumbs over the macaroni and add the remaining shredded cheese on top. Bake at 350 degrees for 25-30 minutes.

$1,000,000

$500,000

$250,000

$100,000

$50,000

$25,000

...st fireworks were invented ... the 7th century in what country?
Answer: China

What year was the 19th Amendment ratified? (Women Suffrage)
Answer: 1920

...at year did High School ...sical come out?

What are the four main ingredients in beer?
Answer: Grai...

Are You Smarter Than a 5th Grader?™

Online trivia questions
Paper
Pencils
Game pieces for markers
Score board printed with dollar amounts up to $1,000,000

Lexi looked up trivia questions online and acted as the host for this game. She printed off questions and cut them into small squares. She created a game board that was a pyramid with values from $1,000 to $1,000,000. We each had the chance to copy or peek at another player's answer. We had to answer correctly to advance on the board.

Tania Tip

This game has few pieces, so it can be comfortably played in any room or even outside.

20 minutes **4-6** players

Planning Ahead

Bacon-Wrapped Sausages
Prep Time: 10 minutes
Cook Time: 30 minutes
Servings: 6-8

Bagel French Toast
Prep Time: 10-15 minutes
Cook Time: 5 minutes
Servings: 2-3

Night Nine: Breakfast for Dinner

Bacon-Wrapped Sausages

2 packages Italian sausage (mild)
10 strips bacon, uncooked
¼ - ½ cup brown sugar
¼ cup maple syrup

Wrap bacon around Italian sausages. Place into a 9 x 13 baking dish. Sprinkle with brown sugar and drizzle with maple syrup. Bake at 350 degrees for about 30 minutes.

Bagel French Toast

2 cinnamon bagels
3 eggs
½ cup milk
½ teaspoon cinnamon
Powdered sugar

Bread slice the bagels. Beat the eggs in a bowl and add milk and cinnamon. Dip both sides of the bagel slices into the egg mixture. Place in a skillet over medium heat. Cook for 1-2 minutes until the bottom is golden brown. Flip and cook the other side for 1 minute. Serve with butter and sprinkle with powdered sugar.

Mimosa

4 ounces champagne
3 ounces pineapple or orange juice
Fresh fruit

Pour juice into a champagne flute. Top with champagne. Add any kind of fresh fruit as a garnish. Makes one serving.

CLASSIC	CHOP! CHOP!	FORE!
$200	$200	$200
$400	$400	$400
$600	$600	$600
$800	$800	$800

Jeopardy™

Jeopardy™ questions
Index cards
Cardboard

Arren and Anni recreated the game Jeopardy™ by looking up questions from a website. Questions were written on index cards and taped to a piece of cardboard. The object of the game is to earn the most money by answering questions correctly. The board had the answers to the questions written on the back. One player began by selecting a category and a value. If they answered the question correctly, they earned the money and could continue to play. If they answered incorrectly, they subtracted the money from their total. The player with the most money at the end wins.

TaniaTip

Choose questions from many different categories to make the game winnable for all.

30 minutes   **2+ players**

Margarita

2 ounces tequila
1 ounce triple sec
1 ounce lime juice
Soda water
Salt

Dip the rim of a margarita glass into lime juice and rim with salt. Add ice to glass. Pour tequila, Triple Sec, soda water, and lime juice into the glass. For a frozen margarita, add the mixture to a blender and blend with 1 cup of ice. Makes one serving.

Night Ten: Southwestern Staycation

BBQ Chicken Tostadas

1 store-bought rotisserie chicken
8-10 street taco tortillas
1 cup BBQ sauce (Use your family's favorite)
Optional toppings: Mozzarella cheese, lettuce, corn, salsa

Preheat the oven to 415 degrees. Spray a baking sheet with cooking spray and lay out the tortillas. Lightly spray the tortillas with the cooking spray. Put in the oven for 5 minutes. Remove.

Remove the meat from the bones of the rotisserie chicken. Shred it with two forks and stir in BBQ sauce.

Put the shredded chicken on the cooked tortillas and top with mozzarella cheese. Bake in the oven for 5 minutes until the cheese is melted. Add your own toppings!

Planning Ahead

BBQ Chicken Tostadas
    Prep Time: 20-30 minutes
    Servings: 5-6

Breaded Zucchini Sticks
    Prep Time: 20-30 minutes
    Cook Time: 10 minutes
    Servings: 5-6

Breaded Zucchini Sticks

2 zucchinis
1 cup Italian breadcrumbs
1 cup flour
2-4 egg whites

Ranch Dipping Sauce
1 cup Greek nonfat plain yogurt
1 packet Ranch dressing seasoning

Breaded Zucchini Sticks
Wash and slice the zucchini to make 5-6 zucchini sticks around ½ inch thick and 4 inches long.

Create a breading station by putting the flour in one dish, the egg whites in a second dish, and the breadcrumbs in a third dish. Roll the zucchini in the flour, then egg whites, and then the breadcrumbs. Bake at 500 degrees for 8 minutes.

Ranch Dipping Sauce
Add 1 packet of ranch dressing seasoning to the Greek yogurt and mix well.

Wheel of Fortune™

Circular disc
Board
Bolt
Screw and washer
Tape
White paper
Markers

30 minutes **4-6 players**

Ron made a spinning wheel out of an old circular saw blade. He attached it to a square board with a screw, a bolt, and a spacer. You could also make this on a paper plate. He divided the blade up into different monetary amounts ($500, $1,000, lose a turn, free spin, etc.). He took large pieces of white paper and drew squares on them for each letter of the word. After we each took a turn by spinning the wheel, we guessed a letter to fill in the puzzle. If you did not select a correct letter for the puzzle, your turn was over. This play continues for each contestant until the puzzle is solved. Ron had three categories for us to play, including people, same name, and places. Then, he hosted a championship round.

51

The End

These were some of the best times I have ever spent with my family. To this day, they still talk about these nights. We really got into the spirit of the games and began to love the competition and secrecy that surrounded our nights together.

These evenings offered us an opportunity to browse through old cookbooks, try new meals, and grow as a family. We were able to broaden our pallettes, challenge our minds, and strengthen our connections.

Above all, I hope you now believe that you can create a night of fun on a budget with items you already have in your home. It is not difficult to create evenings like these for your family or friends. Create a game on your own, pick up a board game, or modify a favorite family game. Dinner or snacks are a must when you plan an event, but you do not have to go overboard or create them all from scratch. Simplify your menu by having a few prepared items and one new recipe.

People will enjoy themselves when there is food, drink, and entertainment provided. It's easy to entertain when you follow these steps. Your guests will be begging you to host again.

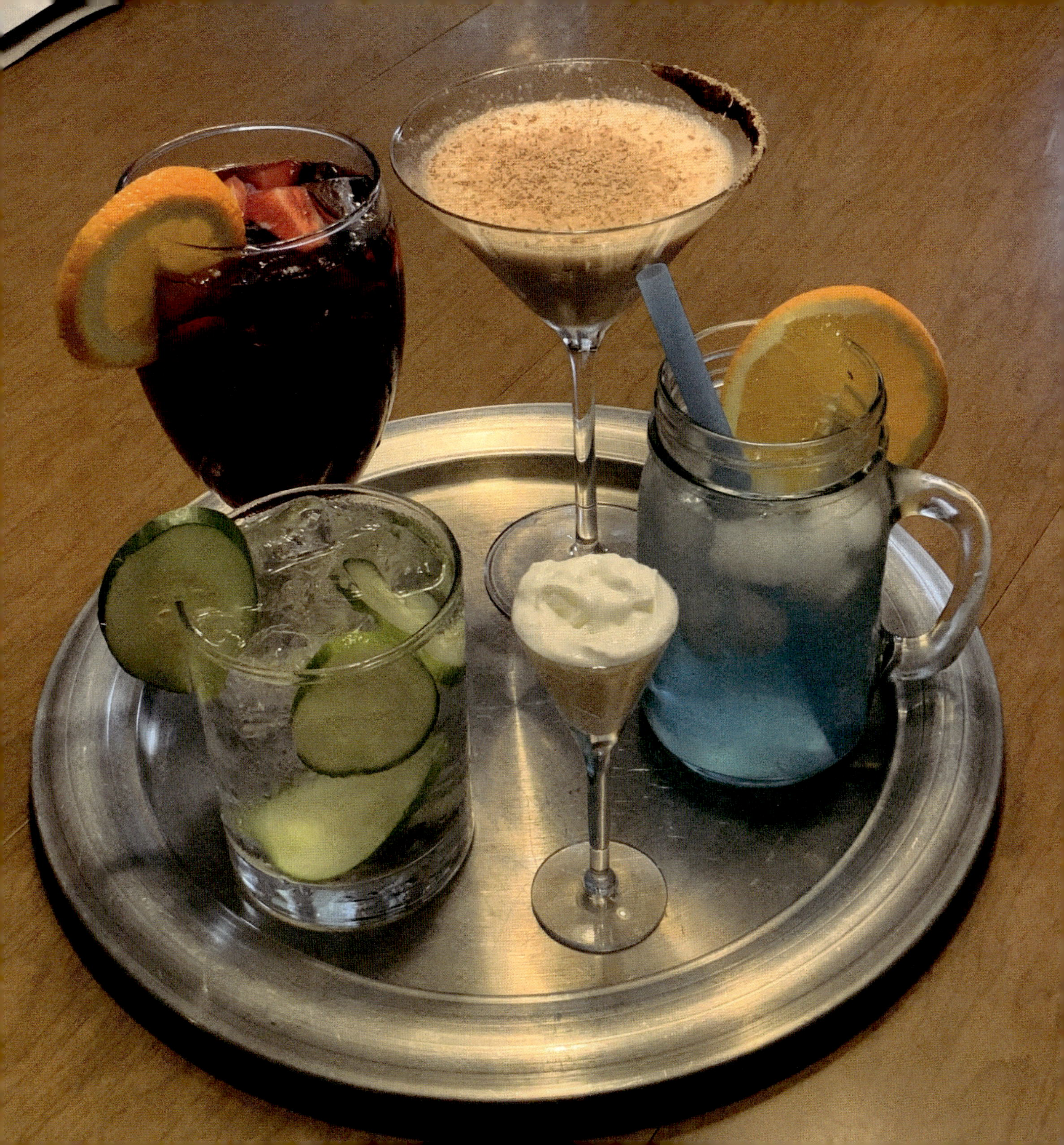

Alternate Recipes

Anni's Pasta

2 kielbasa sausages
1 box (16 ounces) dry bowtie noodles
1 bag mixed vegetables (frozen)
1 cup butter
1 cup parmesan cheese
1 teaspoon garlic powder
1 tablespoon dried parsley
Salt and pepper

Slice and brown the kielbasa sausage. Boil water and cook the bowtie pasta according to the package instructions. Drain. Boil the bag of mixed vegetables and drain. For the sauce, melt the butter in a saucepan. Add the parmesan cheese, parsley, salt, pepper, and garlic powder to the melted butter. Stir to combine. In a large bowl, combine the pasta, sausage, vegetables, and sauce. Sprinkle parmesan cheese over the top. Serves 5-6 people.

Grandma's Potato Salad

4-5 Yukon gold potatoes
1 cup Miracle Whip™
2 celery stalks, diced
½ small onion, diced
3 eggs, boiled and diced
1½ teaspoons celery seed
Salt and pepper

Wash and peel the potatoes. Slice the potatoes in half and then cut into ¼ inch slices. Put the potatoes in a quart sauce pan and cover them with water. Boil the potatoes until they are fork tender. Drain the water and let them cool. In a large bowl, combine diced onions, diced celery, Miracle Whip™, celery seed, salt, and pepper. Add the potatoes and fold gently to mix together. Cover and place in the refrigerator for 4-5 hours or overnight. Serve chilled. Serves 8-10 people.

Spinach and Pepper Frittata

¼ cup each orange, red, and green bell pepper, diced
6 eggs
1 cup fresh spinach
2 tablespoons olive oil
Salt and pepper
Parmesan cheese

Dice bell peppers and chop spinach. Heat the oil in a saucepan. Sauté the peppers in the oil for 2-3 minutes, then add the spinach. Spread the vegetables around the pan to create an even layer. Beat eggs and add salt and pepper. Pour the egg mixture into the pan. Turn the heat down to low and cover for 3-4 minutes. Once the eggs are cooked on the bottom, use a rubber spatula to loosen the sides and let the rest of the eggs run underneath. Cook for 1 minute. Flip the frittata over in the pan. Cook for another 2 minutes. Remove from the pan and sprinkle with parmesan cheese. Serves 4-5 people.

Italian Pasta Salad

1 box (12 ounces) dry pasta of your choice
¼ cup each red, yellow, green, and orange bell pepper, diced
¼ cup onion, diced
1 package broccoli florets
½ - 1 cup Italian dressing
5-10 salami slices
Parmesan cheese
Salt and pepper

Dice bell peppers and onion. Wash and chop the broccoli florets into bite-sized pieces. Cook the pasta according to package instructions. Drain and allow noodles to cool. In a bowl, mix half the Italian dressing into the noodles. Then, add the vegetables, salami, and remaining Italian dressing. Mix in parmesan cheese. Cover and refrigerate for 3-4 hours or overnight. Serve chilled. Serves 8-10 people.

Zesty Lemon Herb Chicken Legs

1 package chicken legs
2 tablespoons dried cilantro
2 tablespoons dried parsley
½ cup olive oil
1 teaspoon salt
1 teaspoon pepper
¼ cup balsamic vinegar
¼ cup red wine vinegar
½ cup water
1 lemon, juice and zest

To make the marinade, combine the cilantro, parsley, olive oil, salt, pepper, balsamic vinegar, red wine vinegar, lemon juice, lemon zest, and water into a gallon size plastic bag. Add the thawed chicken legs to the bag and zip it shut. Roll the chicken legs around in the marinade. Let marinate for at least 15-30 minutes. Place in a baking dish and bake at 375 degrees for 35 minutes. Serves 4-5 people.

Bagel Bruschetta

2 cinnamon bagels
1 package (8 ounces) cream cheese, softened
Fresh fruit
Optional: 1-2 tablespoons honey

Bread slice a cinnamon bagel and toast the slices. Spread cream cheese on it and top with chopped fruit. Drizzle with honey if desired.

Made in the USA
Monee, IL
18 January 2021